Tarleton Brown

Memoirs of Tarleton Brown

A captain of the revolutionary army

Tarleton Brown

Memoirs of Tarleton Brown
A captain of the revolutionary army

ISBN/EAN: 9783337083212

Printed in Europe, USA, Canada, Australia, Japan

Cover: Foto ©ninafisch / pixelio.de

More available books at **www.hansebooks.com**

PROCEEDINGS

AT A

SPECIAL MEETING

OF

The Survivors' Association

OF CHARLESTON DISTRICT.

25TH, 1890,

"The Defense of Charleston Harbor."

PRINTED FOR THE ASSOCIATION BY THE WALKER, EVANS & COGSWELL
COMPANY—1890.

PROCEEDINGS

SPECIAL MEETING

OF

The Survivors' Association,

OF CHARLESTON DISTRICT.

JULY 25TH, 1890,

———————

"The Defense of Charleston Harbor."

———————

PRINTED FOR THE ASSOCIATION

BY THE

WALKER, EVANS & COGSWELL COMPANY.

1890.

A CONFEDERATE EPIC.

MAJOR JOHN JOHNSON'S HISTORY OF "THE DEFENSE OF CHARLESTON HARBOR"—COMPLIMENTARY PREAMBLE AND RESOLUTIONS OF THE SURVIVORS' ASSOCIATION—CAPT. JOHN C. MITCHEL; HIS VENERABLE MOTHER REMEMBERED.

PROCEEDINGS.

In deference to the very general desire of many members, that the Association should be called together specially, in order that some formal action might be taken, to give expression to the gratification of the members upon the publication of the grand historic work by the Rev. John Johnson, "The Defense of Charleston Harbor," a meeting was held in the armory of the Washington Light Infantry on Friday evening, 26th July, and was a large and influential gathering of Survivors.

Col. Zimmerman Davis, President, occupied the chair, and Mr. J. W. Ward acted as Secretary. The meeting was opened by the following address by the President:

Comrades: There has recently been issued from the press a book by one of our townsmen, the Rev. John Johnson, which will be read with absorbing interest in every part of the civilized globe. It graphically but truthfully describes the siege and defense of Charleston harbor during the years 1863-65. It is the history of the unsuccessful attempts of a powerful enemy, backed by unlimited numbers and every appliance then known in the art of war, to capture Charleston and its defenses.

But it is far more than this: it is the history of the most gallant defense of a beleaguered city ever made in the world, in ancient or modern times. It describes the courage and fortitude of its defenders, the trials, the hardships and the privations they endured; the ingenuity and skill they displayed with the limited resources at their command:

their sleepless vigilance; their exalted patriotism; their unconquerable determination that hostile foot should never tread the streets of this beautiful city so long as they held the keys to its gates. This magnificent defense stands without a parallel in the world's history.

We honor these brave defenders; we are proud of them; we are proud of their names and of their fame. And we honor the Historian of these glorious deeds. Being himself one of the most efficient in this grand defense, he has unwittingly crowned himself with additional laurels by perpetuating the story. His book should be in every Southern—yea in every American home. It ought to be read by every man, woman and child in our Southland, and remotest posterity ought to be taught from its thrilling narrative the story of Sumter and Moultrie and Wagner.

In obedience to a widely expressed desire I have called you together this evening that we may consult how best to thank the author of this book, and to express to him our appreciation and gratification for the thoroughness of his work, and its invaluable contribution to the history of our times.

Capt. Wm. A. Courtenay said:

Mr. President and Fellow-members: This is an unusual gathering of the Survivors' Association of Charleston. It has been suggested by an unusual occurrence, the publication of the complete historic narrative of the "Defense of Charleston Harbor."

Twenty-five years have passed since the close of the war: since the last shotted gun was fired in this harbor. During all this long period there has been the yearning that the matchless record of these eventful days be prepared and preserved, not only in justice to the actors in this fierce drama of war at the portals of our city, but as well that posterity should learn on authority, of the unflinching fortitude and the costly sacrifice which illumine these days of severest trial, and which have won a world-wide renown for these sandy shores. Difficulty was Opportunity indeed.

"Worthy deeds," says Milton, "are not often destitute of worthy relators, as by a certain fate great acts and great eloquence have most commonly gone hand in hand, equalling and honoring each other in the same age." How happy then the coincidence with us, that one who held no exalted rank, and was yet a distinguished actor in these stirring times, should become the historian of these warlike events; should have gathered up quietly, the scattered materials of this wonderful defense, preserved them through all these long years, and finally placed this thrilling narrative in elegant and complete form before his native city and State, the South and the Union.

It is a high privilege to be the historian of an eventful epoch; it is easy to heighten the common, to magnify the rare and superior virtues, but our townsman has reached to higher achievement; he has not only recorded the physical features of the exhausting contest with impartial pen, but he has brought the past back to us, and we hear again the pathetic and heroic story which touched our earlier life with wonder and awe. He has done more than this: he has summoned from that fast receding past, the spirit behind the physical forces, wielding the instruments and compelling the events, which lift up this giant struggle to its recognized high place in military history. "Our vigor is now feeble, our grasp uncertain, our stiffest muscle limp, beside the unyielding grapple of those tough wills."

From the impartial pen of the Chief Engineer of Fort Sumter, always our honored townsman, now the Rev. John Johnson, we have the first complete history of so protracted a struggle,—two years of war history.—

"Never on earthly anvil
Had such rare armor gleamed."

The story so graphically told is by one from civil life who, as a junior officer of engineers, transformed this outpost while under fire and thus made it possible to "hold the fort;" whose merit promoted him to be Major of Engineers, one of a very few, elevated to that high rank from civil life.

The energizing spirit of the struggle was reflected in the community in whose presence this contest was waged; an unprepared community, suddenly confronted with serious necessities, involving the highest scientific knowledge, the most complex mechanical skill. In this volume we are told how the first use of iron armor was tested in this harbor, and when this new military idea went forth, and the workshops of the world were taxed to develop and perfect it, and when, in its advanced and perfect form, it was subsequently arrayed against us, how native skill changed old-type smooth-bore ordnance into rifled guns, equal to the defeat and partial destruction of the largest ironclad fleet and the heaviest concentration of ordnance the world had then witnessed.

All honor to the citizen, soldier, author, who has patiently, through all these years, worked to this end, and though repeatedly discouraged, has now finally achieved such great success.

One of the simplest and, to me, most impressive memorials in Westminster Abbey is a marble bust erected in honor of George Grote, with its laconic inscription, " The Historian of Greece."

We have no Parian marble, nor monumental hall, with which to celebrate our historian, but it is equally our duty and privilege to place on record our sincere appreciation of such distinguished services, and as well to preserve to posterity the assurance of our affectionate regard. Be it, therefore,

Resolved, That the warmest thanks of the Survivors' Association of Charleston District are eminently due, and are hereby unanimously tendered, to the Rev. John Johnson for his untiring labors and conspicuous literary ability in writing this grand history of the Confederate struggle in this harbor.

Resolved, That this Association has noticed with disappointment the absence in this volume, of a portrait of the Author and Engineer; that it is due to the completeness of the volume that this omission be forthwith corrected. That the President request the Rev. John Johnson to give his consent for such portrait to be prepared at once and inserted in all copies of the work.

The resolutions were seconded by Gen. Huguenin, he said:

It has always been a source of deep pride and great satisfaction to me, to remember that I had the good fortune and great honor, to have been intimately connected with the Defense of Charleston Harbor from the beginning to the end. Consequently, I am familiar with many of the details of that defense as related in Maj. Johnson's book, not only as a participant, but as one who being at hand, took a great interest in the stirring scenes being enacted by others. The accuracy and historical value of the work I do most unhesitatingly commend; its literary value is without question. The justice which is meted out to " friend and foe " must be admired by all. It must be observed however, that in the nature of things and the natural modesty of the author, sufficient justice has not been done in the volume to the defense of Fort Sumter from an engineering standpoint. It may be true, that " conscience makes cowards of us all," yet I have always believed that man is naturally a courageous animal, when he believes he is in the right and doing his duty to himself or his country. Therefore while the officers and soldiers of Sumter have been justly and fully commended for that gallant defense in the line of duty, yet I have always maintained, and do now assert, that sufficient praise and credit has never been given, in proportion, to the engineers whose great skill, bravery and untiring labor rendered Sumter impregnable. Of these engineers, the first and foremost was Capt. John Johnson, and I have no hesitation in saying, that to him, more than any one else, the credit of its defense is due. Courage undirected by intelligence frequently wastes its energies in fruitless sacrifice, while the cool and intelligent soldier takes advantage of every favorable incident, and turns defeat into victory. All honor then to the skill, energy and courage of him, who himself has most signally proved that " *Difficulty is Opportunity*."

He was followed by Major Theodore G. Barker. Major Barker said :

I esteem it an honor and privilege of no ordinary measure and character to be called on to second the resolutions which have just been read.

It is within the past fortnight that I received my subscription copy of the record of the " Defense of Charleston Harbor." It was at a time when the depression caused by the humiliating spectacle of the recent campaign meetings weighed heavily upon the spirit, when we were told by the men who claimed to speak for the farmers of South Carolina, those whom we have been taught from childhood to believe are the bone and sinew of the State, those whom we had known in the glorious days of 1860 to 1865, and of 1876, as the true and tried sons of South Carolina, proud of her heritage and glory, proud of her history and of their own share in that history, when we were told that these men had united in declaring that all the past of South Carolina was worthless; a barren record of political and social tyranny; a story of wrong and oppression, and a matter of shame rather than of just pride for her children to look upon; it was under this depression, which each morning's newspaper increased and intensified, with the sense of mortification and almost despair, that I opened the record which Major Johnson had prepared of the defense of Charleston.

It is the only book on the war which I have allowed myself to read since the war. I had put away all such reading for the evening of life, when the harness of work shall be laid aside, and the narrative of disappointed hopes can be read in retrospect, with the philosophy of old age to temper the bitterness of regret. Having been absent from the State and from the city of Charleston from May of 1861 to August of 1865, I had known of the heroic defense of Charleston only through the meagre and suppressed accounts which the newspapers were permitted to give, and such casual allusions as came from private letters or conversation.

I confess, the story of concentrated heroism which Major Johnson's book contains was a surprise and revelation to me. I found myself at once charmed and fascinated. Night after night I drank from those pages as from a cool, refreshing fountain, the draughts of purifying, elevating inspiration. I felt that the South Carolina which I had thought I owned as a thing of glory and ennobling pride and which, in the morning's perusal of the newspaper, I felt had been in a manner stolen from me, was by that record of heroism restored in all its truth and brightness to my assured possession.

I felt that, come what come may, through the ugly and degrading turns of adverse political influences, the place of South Carolina in history, as an object of holy reverence, of sincere respect, of unqualified devotion, was rendered secure beyond peradventure or fear of misrepresentation by that noble record of heroic endurance and exalted courage which the days and nights of trial in Fort Sumter and Battery Wagner alone would forever illustrate. It was indeed a happy fate for those, who by their lives and heroism raised the flag of South Carolina high before the gaze of an admiring world, to have given to posterity so grand, so imperishable a place in history, and next to that happy fate, that glorious privilege of those who fought and died in that grand defense, we must esteem that a supreme good fortune to have been the one of the brave defenders to whose lot was cast the power and the honor of being the one whose pen has recorded the undying glory of the men who fought those forts, and who, by their deeds of valor, placed the name of South Carolina higher in the niche of fame than even she had ever before been placed.

All honor to the Major of Engineers of the Fort Sumter garrison, and all honor to the man the work of whose hands and head, inspired by lofty patriotic devotion to his State, aided so materially to the success of that defense, and whose faithful record will, for all the ages to come, preserve in imperishable words the story of Fort Sumter.

Major W. II. Brawley also seconded the resolutions eloquently :

I second these resolutions, he said, most heartily. This book is a record of great events. The defenders of Fort Sumter are worthy to stand in history alongside those who held the pass at Thermopylæ.

South Carolina has not at any time in her history been lacking in brave men. From the time when the Indians were driven across her borders down through the years when her untrained yeomanry crossed swords with Tarlton's cavalry to the day when the flag of the Palmetto regiment was the first to be planted upon the walls of Mexico, we had before us examples of valor worthy of the heroic ages, so that it was to be expected when our day of trial came that we too knew how to offer our lives for our country. The battlefields of the late war between the States showed that we were not degenerate sons, but it was given to our brothers here at the seaward gates of this old city to carve upon the battered casemates of Fort Sumter a story of chivalry that will survive through all the ages. It is that story that is recorded in this volume. It should be read by our sons and sent down as a precious heritage to those who come after us.

It is wise and well that we should revive the memory of those days, when all the sons of South Carolina stood shoulder to shoulder, at this hour when we are riven by factional and sectional dissension. It is well that we should pause in the mad struggle for place and in the eager pursuit of material good and remember that the names most loved and the memories most revered are of those who have shown that they truly loved the State and were willing to die for her ; that fortitude and fidelity to principle, devotion to country and to great causes contribute most to her permanent fame and glory.

This is peculiarly a time when such memories should be revived. A generation has passed away since the guns at

Sumter were silenced, and men "who knew not Joseph" have come upon the scene.

The preservation of the memories of great deeds is an element and means of attaining greatness. We could not if we would escape our past and if we have the seeds of worthiness in us we would not. Our State has done wisely therefore in subscribing for a hundred copies of this volume, and in directing that they be distributed among our schools and colleges, for while there are a few among us who are ready to plead the Statute of Limitations against all claims growing out of the services and sacrifices therein recorded, so long as we preserve our self respect as a people, the eye will moisten, and the tongue will tremble, as those memories are recalled.

While the story of the Defense of Charleston is the most unique and brilliant page in our history, let us hope that its wide circulation will be the incentive and forerunner of other histories of deeds not less glorious though less known.

The ever thinning ranks of our Survivors warn us that it is time to put into permanent record those memories we would not willingly let die.

Gen. George D. Johnston, late Superintendent of, the South Carolina Military Academy, said he responded in part as a South Carolinian, and in part as the representative of another Confederate State. He was glad that this last opportunity, before leaving South Carolina, was afforded him to speak in behalf of this production of Confederate history, and to say a word in reference to the Confederate record of this glorious little State. During the war he had not the privilege to serve here. He was first in the Army of Northern Virginia, and later in the Army of the Tennessee, but he knew what the feeling of Charleston's defenders were. The eyes of all the Southern armies were constantly turned to Charleston to know how well the guns were being served. We knew that if the defenses were once broken and the coast exposed the Confederacy would be split in twain. But they felt that Charleston was in safe hands; and while they took care of their own front, South Carolina protected the rear and the flanks. He had read the book with great profit, interest and entertainment, and it was an epic in Confederate history, showing examples of heroism which had their counterpart only at Thermopylæ. It was the calmest and most dispassionate work on the war he had ever seen, and it was a book that would live, and should be placed on the shelves of every library in the South.

He heartily seconded the Resolutions.

Col. S. B Pickens said:

Mr. President and Comrades:

I regret that circumstances have prevented me from being prepared to second these Resolutions in more fitting terms. I endorse most heartily all that has been said in commendation of this grand work on the Defense of Charleston Harbor. This book of Major Johnson's supplies what has long been wanted in order to form a just conception of the heroic defense of Fort Sumter and other Forts and Batteries around Charleston. It was my fortune to be a Lieutenant in Castle Pinckney during the bombardment of Fort Sumter in 1861, which resulted in the surrender of that Fort by Major Anderson, without the loss of a single life on either side. Those of us who shortly afterwards went to Virginia and witnessed the tremendous clash of arms in open field, with fearful slaughter, were unable to appreciate the dangers and severe trials of our comrades in the Forts, when the tremendous power of iron clad fleets and land batteries were concentrated against them. While on wounded furlough, I came to Charleston, and by permission of Gen. Beauregard went one night to Fort Sumter and had the opportunity of seeing the effects of the terrific bombardment, and could well form an idea of the heroism and great fortitude of officers and men who were under this terrific fire night and day, performing the most trying and continuous duties, of which, those of us in the field, had not a just conception.

I feel, therefore, that not only those who participated in this defense, but every Southern soldier owes to Major Johnson a debt of gratitude for giving to us this book, and that it should be read by every Survivor, and handed down as a precious legacy to our children.

In Memoriam.

Capt. Courtenay, addressing the Chair, said:

Mr. President, there is a grave in our beautiful City of the Dead, which Carolina's daughters yearly deck with flowers on Memorial Day, and on which stands an enduring gray granite monument erected many years ago, by friends who loved the exile's gallant son, and who inscribed upon it this record:

JOHN C. MITCHEL,

Captain 1st regiment S. C. Artillery, C. S. A.,
Commanding Fort Sumter.
Killed upon the parapet during the bombardment.
July 20, 1864.   Aged 26.

" I willingly give my life for South Carolina ;
Oh that I could have died for Ireland."
[His last words.]

Erected by his Comrades, 1878.

There lives in a distant city a venerable matron, with brow frosted by time, whose gracious smile is a benediction, and whose thoughts instinctively wander back to this Southland. She gave three sons to the war; one made the last sacrifice at Gettysburg; another on the ramparts of Sumter, and the third, her only surviving son, bears on his person honorable scars won in that contest. On such an occasion as this, every survivor is moved in heart by such mention, and it has occurred to me that it would be a satisfaction to us all, if we could, in an unobtrusive way, and with filial reverence, renew to the mother of our dead soldier friend the assurance of our sympathy after the lapse of twenty-six years. I am sure that such united action would be a solace to this dear lady in her saddened home, and with this purpose I suggest that a copy of the " Defense of Charleston," handsomely bound and suitably inscribed be presented to Mrs. Jane Verner Mitchel.

And I further suggest that a committee of five, to consist of our President as chairman, the Rev. John Johnson, Capt. Chas. Inglesby, of Capt. Mitchel's company, Gen. McCrady and Capt. James Armstrong, be requested to carry out these wishes of the Association.

On motion of Capt. Wm. Aiken Kelly the name of Capt. Courtenay was added to the committee by a unanimous vote.

In seconding the resolution Capt. Charles Inglesby said:

Mr. President: In the summer of 1861 I received my commission as Lieutenant of Artillery in the regular army of South Carolina. From that time until his death John C. Mitchel and I were officers in the same command, which, upon the formation of the Southern Confederacy, was mustered into the Confederate army and its officers commissioned by the Confederate Government. Under our organization, we were regimental and not company officers. In the fall of 1863, regimental promotions assigned me to Capt. Mitchel's company as his senior first lieutenant, and it was then that the pleasant relations existing between us ripened into a warm and intimate personal friendship. So far as I know, every officer in the regiment esteemed and respected him: most certainly I did. But it was not until I became his senior lieutenant, occupying the same tent with him at Fort Johnson, under the constant fire of the enemy's batteries on Morris Island, that I was able to take in the whole measure of the man. It is my deliberate judgment that, for his years, he was one of the most remarkable men that I have ever known.

As an officer and soldier he possessed the highest military qualifications, while no braver or more gallant officer ever flashed a sword. At the same time, his heroic and daring spirit never made him forget the caution and prudence which an intelligent commander should observe with reference to the safety of those under him.

As a man, his was the highest standard of honor and courtesy, and as a scholar it has ever been a profound mystery to me, how so young a man could have acquired so much knowledge. An accomplished mathematician, his amusement was to work out the most difficult problems in calculus. A wonderful historian; he was thoroughly versed in English and especially in Irish History. He was a fair classical scholar, and at the same time could make himself understood in three or four modern languages.

With the strictest views of right and wrong, he reverenced and respected all that was worthy of reverence and respect; no one ever heard him scoff at religion, and he regarded woman with the chivalrous deference of a knight of the olden time. He espoused the Southern Cause, because he felt that in doing so, he was not only battling for the right, but was defending the weak against the arrogance of power! Small in stature and of delicate physique, he was in heart, soul and intellect a giant!

He was detached from his company January 4, 1864, and placed in command of Fort Sumter—from this until his death he was never again in immediate command of the company, although it was our pleasure to serve several tours of duty under him at that post. We were at Battery Marion on Sullivan's Island when the news of his death reached us on 20th July, 1864, and men as well as officers, felt that we had not only lost a captain and leader in whom we absolutely relied, but we had also lost a comrade whom we all dearly loved. His death placed the third bar on my collar, but feeling that I had lost "a friend who was nearer than a brother," the happiness of promotion was lost in grief for the death of my friend!

As I have said, I was at my post on Sullivan's Island when he received his death wound and died in Fort Sumter. It was, therefore, not permitted me to be with him in his last hours, but those who were, bear witness that he died the gallant hero that he lived. Some time afterwards, I accidentally heard two soldiers who had been in the fort at the time, speaking of him. They were utter strangers to me and were not talking for effect. The one said to his comrade: "Do you know why it was that Capt. Mitchel was killed"? Upon being asked, why, he replied: "Because he did not know that Yankee shells could hurt anybody. No matter how the shot and shells were flying, he would walk about and not seem to know that there was any danger in them."

It was the pride of the South, that her armies were composed of her own people and not of the hirelings from all parts of the world, as were the armies of the North. Comparatively few foreigners fought beneath the Southern Cross. Those who did, were sons of freedom who came to fight for freedom's cause! He was one of those. And no life-blood shed in our war came from a truer, purer, nobler heart than that which came from the heart of John C. Mitchel.

I second the resolutions.

Col. Edward McCrady, Jr., spoke as follows:

Mr. Chairman: I shall gladly act upon the committee suggested by Capt. Courtenay. The names of Lafayette,

DeKalb and Steuben—men from other lands who came to America to fight for her independence—are preserved throughout the land. The struggle for freedom in which they took part was successful, and a grateful country has perpetuated their memories in the names of its cities, counties, forts and societies.

The struggle for constitutional liberty in which Capt. Mitchel fell, was unsuccessful, but none the less should we, in whose cause he gave up his life a voluntarily sacrifice, gratefully remember his heroism and honor his name. True 'tis little we can do in his honor, but that little may be priceless in touching the heart of the aged mother still grieving for her gallant son. It will, at least, gratify her to know that the people of the old city for whom he fought and fell, have not forgotten his deeds, nor the sacrifice in giving so precious a life in their cause; that we, the survivors of the army in which he fought, think of his mother, and sympathize alike in her pride and her grief, as we read the admirable story of Fort Sumter and the conspicuous part Capt. Mitchel bore in the glorious defense, and of his heroic death upon its crumbling walls.

The resolutions were also seconded by Capt. James Armstrong.

The chaste and tender tribute, he said, to the courage and fidelity of the three sons of the Irish patriot and devoted friend of the South, John Mitchel, which has just been offered by Capt. Courtenay, and the delicate and deserved compliment he wishes to confer on their noble mother, not only receives our hearty approval, but will also elicit the admiration of the race to which these self-sacrificing heroes belonged. This mourning mother, who like Sparta of old, estimated her wealth by the virtue and valor of her children, will value this precious souvenir more highly than if it were gold, for it eloquently and truthfully tells of the incomparable siege of Charleston in which one of her sons, Capt. John C. Mitchel, displayed the very chivalry of courage, exhibited sublime fortitude, and died a glorious death. This history will be doubly dear to her, for it has been written by one who was a courageous comrade and dear friend of her son, who fell while in command of Fort Sumter, on the 375th day of the siege. In his official announcement of the fact that John C. Mitchel was mortally wounded, Major Johnson, Engineer Officer of the Fort, added: 'Alas, what a loss!' The Charleston Courier of July 21, 1864, in noticing Capt. Mitchel's death, mentioned how strongly he was attached to Major Johnson said :

" He spoke with special enthusiasm concerning the fidelity, courage, devotion and energy of Capt. Johnson of the engineers as largely entitled to credit for the defense of Fort Sumter, and also concerning the cool and deliberate determination of the garrison to defend and replace, when needed, the flag which had so often been cut down but never lowered or kept down."

Capt. Armstrong continued : I earnestly hope that the suggestion of Capt. Courtenay may be adopted, and I trust that his name will be added to the committee.

Capt. Courtenay's proposal was unanimously adopted, after which the meeting adjourned.

ZIMMERMAN DAVIS,
President.

From the Minutes.
J. W. WARD,
Secretary.

CONFEDERATE THOUGHTS.

The proceedings of the Survivors' Association last evening are marked by excellence in every respect. The eulogium pronounced on Rev. John Johnson's history of the Defense of Charleston," does credit to all concerned and will be satisfying to the whole community; no home in South Carolina or in all our Southland, and as for that, no impartial home in the Union, should be without this grand chapter of American War history, while the military student everywhere will not fail to study this full and remarkable lesson of war.

The remembrance of the Mitchel family will touch every heart, where this most worthy mention is read.

Mr. John Mitchel, the exile, upon reaching the United States, lived in the South, and his vigorous and scholarly pen was wielded warmly for Southern rights.

When the war came on, his eldest son, John C. Mitchel, came quickly to Charleston soon after the ordinance of secession was passed, and through Judge Magrath's influence, was early commissioned by Governor Pickens as second lieutenant of the First South Carolina regular Artillery.

His soldierly qualities so attracted Gen. Beauregard's notice, that on the transfer of Gen. Elliott from Fort Sumter to Virginia this youthful captain of artillery was appointed to the command of Fort Sumter, where he lost his life in the discharge of his duty. His younger brother, William H. Mitchel was at school in France when the war begun, but ran the blockade, volunteered "for the war" in a Virginia corps, and fell, storming the heights of Gettysburg in Pickett's famous charge—barely 18 years of age. A third and only surviving son, Capt. James Mitchel, also entered the Confederate army in a Virginia regiment, was severely wounded, but still survives and lives in New York, where his mother and only sister also reside.

Nearly three decades have gone by since these events happened, and it is to the honor of Charleston that her Survivors' Association recalls these costly sacrifices in a single family which, in perilous times, cast their lot so unselfishly with our Southland. The delicate and respectful attention to the venerable Mrs. Mitchel will find an approving response not only here, but wherever it becomes known in South Carolina and the South. It is a pleasure to record so thoughtful an act.

"To live in hearts
We leave behind is not to die."

[*Charleston, S. C., World, 26th July.*]

CHARLESTON, S. C., July 26th, 1890.

DEAR MRS. MITCHEL:

The Survivors' Association of this city has appointed us a special Committee to transmit to you herewith their Resolutions of July 25th, 1890, accompanied with an inscribed copy of the historical work, entitled: "*The Defense of Charleston Harbor, &c.*," and to ask your acceptance of the same.

It is a truthful narrative of the times of difficulty, trial and danger; and we are fully sensible of the fact that your lot was cast with us, and that your tenderest ties of motherhood were shared with the matrons of the soil, in gladly giving as they did, your noblest offspring to the cause of the Southern Confederacy. While many of these Spartan mothers were permitted to welcome home their heroic sons returning from the war and bringing back their untarnished shields with them, we gratefully and sorrowfully remember that your noble son, Captain John C. Mitchel, while at his post of duty as commander of the proudest citadel of our harbor, was stricken down by the foe and borne back from the forefront of battle upon his equally bright and untarnished shield. Placed in command of this fortress, the outpost of the harbor and the gateway to the city, he justified all the faith and confidence which his adopted State and country had in him, and now his remains are resting in our own soldiers' ground.

While we, his comrades of the war, preserve in our hearts the record of his gallant services before our once beleagured city, let us hope that you will admit into the shrine of your memory, as watchers with you at the tomb of that dear son, those whose names are signed below. Invoking the Divine favor upon you and your family, we assure you of our abiding affection and remain,

Your obedient servants,
ZIMMERMAN DAVIS, *President.*
JNO. JOHNSON.
CHARLES INGLESBY.
EDWARD McCRADY, JR.
JAMES ARMSTRONG.
WM. A. COURTENAY.

NEW YORK, August 6th, 1890.

Col. Zimmerman Davis
    and Gentlemen of the Committee, Charleston, S. C.

DEAR SIRS—I have just received your communication on behalf of the Survivors' Association, and hasten to assure you of my deep gratitude to you and your associates, and to the good people of Charleston, for this thoughtful and gracious act of kindness towards myself and those few members of my family still left to me. If anything could compensate me for the heavy losses I have sustained, it would be the knowledge that there are many who have shared my grief with me, and that the worth and services of my son are recognized, and his memory borne in affectionate remembrance by those with whom he was so closely associated, who knew him well in the days when all were so sorely tried.

I need hardly say how highly I value Mr. Johnson's book and the proceedings of the Association. They will be preserved among my most cherished mementoes of our great War, among which is a little pencil sketch by the author of this history, of a casemate in Fort Sumter, sent me soon after my son's death.

Hoping gentlemen, to be permitted at some time or other to visit your noble city, and there to have the pleasure of meeting you, and of again personally telling you how deeply I have have been touched by your kindness,

I am, with sincere regard very truly yours,

JANE MITCHEL.

MEMOIRS

OF.........

TARLETON
BROWN

Written by Himself

BARNWELL, S. C., 15th April 1895.

My Dear Holmes:

I acknowledge with thanks the copy of Tarleton Brown's Memoirs which you sent me. It is a most valuable contribution to local history.

The original was dictated by Mr. Brown to C. C. Hay, Esq., who married his grand-daughter, Miss Peyton, and published in pamphlet form during Brown's life. I had a copy, which was lost, greatly to my regret, and have sought unsuccessfully to replace it. Your reprint nearly a half century later is timely and no doubt will gratify others as much as myself; for apart from its historic interest I doubt if any man of his day has more of his blood in the present population of Barnwell County than Tarleton Brown.

He lived to be nearly a hundred years old, and in my childhood I remember to have seen him, and recall the consideration in which he was held by the people and to which his services had entitled him.

JOHNSON HAGOOD.

John W. Holmes, Esq., Ed. of *People*.

MEMOIRS

OF

TARLETON BROWN,

A Captain in the Revolutionary Army,

WRITTEN BY HIMSELF.

- -

BARNWELL, S. C.
THE PEOPLE PRESS.
1894.

MEMOIRS.

M Y father, William Brown, was a planter in Albemarle County, Virginia, where I was born on the 5th day of April, 1757. Flattering inducements being held forth to settlers in the rich region of South Carolina contiguous to the Savannah River; and my uncle, Bartlet Brown, having already moved, and settled himself two miles above Matthew's Bluff, on the Savannah River; my father brought out some negroes. and left them with his brother to make a crop; and in 1769, a year afterwards, my father and family, consisting of eleven persons, emigrated to this country and settled on Brier's Creek, opposite to Burton's Ferry. We found the country in the vicinity very thinly inhabited. Our own shelter for several weeks to protect us from the weather was a bark tent, which served for our use until we could erect a rude dwelling of logs.

Having cleared a piece of land, we planted, and found the soil to be exceedingly fertile in the river swamp, producing abundant crops. The country was literally infested with wild beasts, which were very annoying to the inhabitants—killing the stock and destroying the crops—and were so bold, daring, and ravenous, that they would come into our yards, and before our doors take our sheep and poultry. Indeed, it was dangerous to venture out at night beyond the precincts of our yards unarmed. We used every device to exterminate them, and ultimately effected our object by setting traps and poisoned bait.

The forest abounded with all kinds of game, particularly deer and turkeys—the former were almost as gentle as cattle. I have seen fifty together, in a day's ride in the woods. The latter were innumerable, and so very fat that I have often run them down on horseback. The range for cattle was excellent; it was a very common thing to see two hundred in a gang in the large ponds. In any month in the year beeves in the finest order for butchering might be obtained from the forest. It was customary then to have large pens or enclosures for cattle under the particular charge or direction of some person or persons; I was informed by one of those who kept a pen at King Creek, that there had been marked that spring seven hundred calves. Our produce for market was beef, pork, staves, and shingles. There was but little corn planted in that section then; and, indeed, there was scarcely any inducement to plant more than sufficed for our own consumption, there being but few mills in the country, and consequently very little demand for the article.

From the fact of the new and unsettled state of the country, it may readily be inferred that the roads were very inferior; in truth, they were not much better than common bridle paths; and I feel confident in asserting that there were not, in the whole Barnwell District, any conveyances superior to carts of common wood slides. There were a great many wild horses running at large in the forest when we first settled in the district, a number of which were caught and sold by various individuals, who pursued exclusively the business for a livelihood.

In 1775 the war broke out in South Carolina, and troops were required for the service—a draft was accordingly ordered in our section, and being one among the drawn number, we forthwith took up the line of march for Pocotaligo, then under command of General Bull, where we were stationed about seven weeks. Nothing of importance requiring our attendance at that place, our company was discharged, and we returned to our homes, where we had scarcely arrived, when another draft was ordered, for the first siege of Savannah, Georgia. On this occasion I escaped being drawn, but was employed by William Bryant to act in his place.

We embarked in an open boat, on the Savannah River, Capt. Moore commanding our company. After three days' passage down the river we arrived at Savannah, in good health and in fine spirits, all eager to engage in the contest, and to assert our rights as freemen through the muzzles of our muskets and at the points of our swords. We passed some heavy and mortal shots at the enemy, which were returned with equal fierceness and more deadly effect. During the heat of the battle, the iron hail pouring in torrents upon our devoted heads, a ball struck me in the breast, but being well nigh spent, it providentially did no other damage than raise a blood blister. We stayed at Savannah about seven weeks, and then returned to South Carolina, under the command of Gen. Bull.

Having now become greatly attached to the army, in April, 1776, I enlisted in the regular service at Fort Littleton, Beaufort District, commanded by that brave and sagacious officer, Capt. William Harden. There were about eighty-five men stationed at Fort Littleton, and I am the only one now remaining of that number. The greater part of the rest, through the fortunes of war, left their bones bleaching upon the battle plains; the few who survived the ravages of war, have long since fallen beneath the cold and relentless hand of death.

In July, 1777, I left Capt. Harden, but immediately joined Col. James Thompson's detachment on Pipe Creek. While stationed there, I accompanied Capt. John Mumford, and a few choice fellows, upon an expedition to Georgia, to take a guard commanded by Capt. Mott, a Tory, near Hutson's Ferry. We thought to surprise them; but, through some unaccountable means, they had discovered our intentions some time before we reached the house where they were barricaded, and snugly encasing themselves, were prepared for our attack, and kept us at bay by firing at us through their port holes. The enemy, from their favorable position, could single out our men with deadly aim.

During the engagement, I screened myself behind a tree, with the twofold object of protecting myself from danger and taking deliberate aim at the enemy. Whilst in the act of shooting, a ball from the fort struck the tree just above my head, and dashed the bark into my face. I was rather cautious how I projected my head again beyond the necessary limits. As our Captain was now severely wounded in the knee, and John Booth mortally, of which he soon died, we gathered our wounded in blankets, and returned to South Carolina, to Col. Thompson's camps. When Charleston fell into the hands of the British, under the command of Sir Henry Clinton and Admiral Arbuthnot, Captain Mumford, in attempting to make his way to the American Army, was attacked at Morris' Ford, Saltketchie, by old Ben John and his gang of Tories. In this encounter the poor fellow lost his life, and a truer patriot and braver soldier never fell. He now sleeps at the foot of a large pine, on the left hand side of the main road to Barnwell C. H., a few rods South of the bridge, just at the turn of the road from which you can see the bridge.

A short time after these misfortunes, being stung to the quick at our recent defeat and irretrievable loss, and thirsting for justice, a company of fifty horse, led by Col. Thompson and Major Bourguoin, sallied forth on a second expedition to take the formidable Captain Mott and his allies. In this instance, fortune favored us. I took part of the company, and went between the house and swamp. Our approach was so quiet and unexpected by the Tories that, making a charge upon them, they, without the least effort to defend themselves, surrendered. Taking our prisoners, we returned in triumph to our headquarters, and from thence they were sent to Charleston under a strong guard.

After this capture of Capt. Mott and his band of Tories, I continued with Capt. Thompson but a short time. Leaving him, in conjunction with Joshua Inman and John Green, I raised a company of horse, which we called the "Rangers," with the view of scouting those sections of the country adjacent to the Savannah River, both in Georgia and Carolina, as occasion required. Our station was at Cracker's Neck, S. C. Whilst there, our rude boys would go out in the back swamp and frolic with the inhabitants, and from the great quantity of pinders they saw among them, said they would give it the name of Pinder Town, by which name it has gone ever since, as it is now well known by the name of "Pinder Town." During our stay at Cracker's Neck, we took two trips to Sunsburry, Midway Settlement, Georgia, under the command of Generals Pickens and Twiggs. We had a fight with the British and Tories on Ogeechee Causeway; but not much damage was sustained on either side.

In one of our trips to Midway, a young man by the name of Richardson went ahead of us for the purpose of advising the enemy of our approach, but there lived a Mr. Cooper upon the road, directly in our route, who had a pretty daughter named Jane; and it was well known that young Richardson was in love with Miss Jane, and we suspected that he would call in to see her; so I selected a few men, and by a shorter way between the house and the swamp, intercepted him. He was, as we conjectured, at Cooper's, and as soon as he heard the approach of our men, he ran out—we fired upon him and left him dead. Cooper ran through an old field, but we sent a few shots after him, one of which entered his heel and stopped him (I think the distance was nearly two hundred yards)—we brought him to the house, and left him with his family.

In our two trips to Georgia, we made a road in it, which since has become a public road, and is now called the "Rebel Road." Georgia, at this time, was completely in the hands of the British and Tories. They often crossed the river, and killed and plundered the Whigs without mercy. On one occasion I visited my father and the family, with the view of remaining with them all night. On arriving at home, I was pleased to find my brother-in-law, John Joice, and a friend from Augusta there, on a visit for a short time, for the times were now dangerous, the Tories having threatened my life and the life of one of my brothers. I felt that in case we were attacked, they might render us essential service. And it so came to pass that on this very night they came to put into execution their threat. It was about midnight when they arrived. I was sleeping in the hall, and was awakened by the barking of the dogs. In a few minutes I was brought to my feet by a loud rap at the door. I asked, "Who's there?" Several voices together replied "Friends," and said that they were from Sister's Ferry. Gen. Lincoln's army—that their term of enlistment had expired, and that they were now on their return home—were greatly fatigued from traveling, and would like to remain with us during the night. I expressed to them my regret at our inability to accommodate them, as our house was filled with company. After a few minutes' secret deliberation, they asked for a torch of fire, and said they would go to Brier's Creek and encamp. I felt disposed to accommodate them as far as practicable, yet I had some misgivings with regard to the truth of the statement they had made; but recollecting that the militia were about to be discharged at that point, my doubts were in a great measure removed. I, therefore, opened the door and handed them a light, but, as if directed by a supernatural agency, I instantly closed it again, and looking through the crack above the door, I could distinctly see what passed among my friends without, by the light of their torch, and to my astonishment I found them to be Tories. Here judge of the narrow escape I made. With what ease they could have put an end to my existence, entered our abode and massacred all within, ere we could have been aroused to a sense of our danger. Coming to the door a second time, they asked for water. I had now discovered the true object of their mission, and was upon my guard. Having made the door doubly fast, I told them in a repulsive tone they might get it out of the well in the yard. This exasperated them exceedingly, and with loud voices they denounced me, father, and all the family, threatening to visit vengeance upon the whole household, and with fiendish fury and united strength endeavored to burst the door from its hinges; but finding they could not, they endeavored to shoot me through the crack (it being a log house, as before mentioned), and they had a tolerable fair chance to do so, as the door of the room in which my father and the family lay was open, and the light shining through it from the room into the hall where I was.

They fired four or five times, but missed me and killed my little brother, who was aroused by the uproar. By this time we had gathered our arms, and they made off some little distance from the house, still firing, but to no effect. We were well supplied with powder and ball, and if they had been men and stood their ground like soldiers (and not have skulked off into the dark as all cowards and villains do when there is an opportunity offered to fight on equal grounds), we would soon have given them what they richly deserved. I have good reason to be thankful to Almighty God for his kind care and protection of me through so many dangers. I can plainly discern a divine interposition in my deliverance from the hands of those prowling murderers and plunderers.

A few months subsequent to this period, I withdrew from the "Rangers" at Cracker's Neck, and connected myself with a company of militia keeping guard at Burton's Ferry. We exchanged shots almost every day with the British and Tories, who were on the opposite side (Georgia). A man moved over and joined our party, who said he had buried three jugs of rum at Hershman's Lake, and designated the spot. One of our number (Benjamin Green) said he knew the place, having once lived in the vicinity of the lake; so being in the right humor for an exploit, we soon devised, and put into execution, a plan for visiting the premises. Benjamin Green, Henry Best, John Colding and myself took a small canoe and proceeded down King Creek to Savannah River; while we were moving up the stream of the river, with every prospect of success in our enterprise, a gang of Tories numbering thirty-five suddenly appeared upon the bank, where they had been lying in ambush, awaiting our approach. They hailed us, swearing that if we did not come to and surrender, they would kill every one of us. But we had too much knowledge of these rascals and their duplicity to be decoyed in that manner, and to trust ourselves to their clemency. We well knew that if we submitted, death would be the inevitable consequence, and, therefore, preferred risking our chance in the little canoe, as there was a possibility of evading their shot. Immediately turning our boat's head, with our united strength we urged her forward toward the opposite shore. At this instant they commenced a heavy firing at us. Best was soon wounded, and instantly leaped into the water, and clung to the side of the canoe; Colding also received several wounds, which disabled him from further assistance, so he laid down in the canoe, and Green by his side. All hopes of success seemed now centered in myself; with the rapidity of thought, I seized the best paddle, seated myself in the stern of the canoe, and moved her forward with astonishing celerity, reaching in a few minutes the land. Whilst paddling, I felt an acute sensation across the back of my neck and shoulders. On reaching the shore, I examined myself, and found that they had put three balls through my clothes, two of which had slightly scarified my flesh. Returning to the ferry, we severally recovered from our wounds, but never felt again a disposition to repeat our expedition. Poor Best and Colding had scarcely entered upon duty again, before they were both killed by some of these very Tories.

On one occasion I was under the necessity of going home on some important business. Soon after my arrival, a company of horse passed directly in front of our residence. My first impression concerning them was that they were a reinforcement of our guard at the ferry. So soon as I had finished my business, I returned with all possible speed, overjoyed at the prospect of an accession to our numbers. On reaching the fort, to my astonishment, I found it completely evacuated. My reinforcement turned out to be a gang of Tories from Jackson's Branch, on the Saltkatchie, commanded by that famous old Tory, Ned Williams. When they rode up to the ferry, the guard took them to be friends, and gave them a cordial reception, congratulating themselves upon so large an addition to their force. They thus unconsciously and ignorantly delivered themselves up to the enemy, and were taken across the river and placed in the hands of a large body of British and Tories, stationed at Harbard's store, about two miles from the ferry. The intelligence of this capture reached Col. Leroy Hammond at Augusta, who, without delay, marched down at the head of an effective force, and slew nearly the whole of the enemy, releasing and returning with the Whig captives to Augusta, from whence my father, who was one among the number taken, came safely home.

The country now seemed to be almost in complete subjugation to the British. Yet had they not been aided and abetted by those unprincipled and bloodthirsty tools; those "fiends incarnate, whom it were a base slander to term men;" I say, had the Tories but shown themselves the genuine sons of America—the uncompromising, unswerving, champions of liberty, bound together by every social and national tie—the enemy would never have gained a solid foothold upon our shores, and tyranny and oppression would sooner have been swept from our land. But how sadly the reverse! They who had grown up "side by side, and hand in hand, together," father, son, and brother, were arrayed in mortal and ferocious strife against each other. The friends of liberty were beset on every hand, and from every quarter, until drawn from their homes and families, with stout hearts and strong arms, they struck

"For their altars and their fires,
God, and their native land."

Eternal vigilance and action were indispensable, by which, and with a firm reliance on the God of battles, they fought, bled, and conquered.

It was seldom, indeed, that I sought the peaceful shades of my home, as a respite from the laborious duties and toils of the service. The enchantments of the family circle exercise an almost uncontrollable influence over the hearts and minds of men, and yet sweet as are the voices of those we love, and strongly as do cling our heart-strings around the objects of our affections, appealing to our sympathies in loud and soul-stirring language, still louder and more imperative is the call of our country to duty, and the soldier rushes precipitately from the charms and delights of the family circle to the call of his country, his heart burning with patriotic zeal for glory.

Such was the state of things at this crisis, and such was the fire which burned in the breast of every Whig of the Revolution.

It was no time for supineness and lamentation—every energy of the soul had to be exercised, for it was the struggle of weakness against strength, of the undisciplined against the disciplined, and of the raw and untutored militia of an infant country with the well trained regulars of an old, experienced, and skillful nation.

With these truths impressed upon my mind, I allowed myself little or no leisure time, and was either engaged in the performance of duty in the camp, or scouting, as circumstaces required. A short time after the capture of our guard at the ferry, I accompanied Col. McCoy, who took command of a small force, on a trip to the Ogeechee River, in Georgia, with the view of attacking a little band of Tories quartered in that vicinity. These we overtook in the woods, before arriving at the rendezvous; a running fight ensued, but from the denseness of the forest we were thwarted in our design, and the Tories made good their escape, for, if my memory serves me correctly, not one of them was killed. Thus frustrated and baffled, we returned to Carolina. On our arrival, we learnt that Capt. James Roberts, who had been scouting with a company on the Edisto River, had (whilst encamping for the night, by some treachery of the Tories,) been delivered into the hands of Col. Chaney and Williams, who cruelly butchered many of his men, Capt. Roberts and the rest escaping only with their lives. For this outrage we determined to have satisfaction. So thirty-six men, myself among the number, immediately volunteered under Capt. Joseph Vince, a fine officer and a brave soldier, to pursue these scoundrels, and to avenge the blood of our brave comrades. We overtook some of their number in what is called the "Fork of Edisto River," upon whom we visited summary and immediate justice, killing five or six. From thence we proceeded to Captain Salley's "Cowpens," a few miles distant. Whilst there our commander rode, unaccompanied, to a mill located near the house of the Pens. Here he was fired upon by several Tories lying in ambush hard by and seriously wounded by musket shot—in consequence of which he was disabled from doing duty for some time. This unfortunate circumstance interrupting our further march, we were compelled to retrace our steps and return to headquarters, Savannah River.

At this time my father's family lived at the Big House, now belonging to Col. Hay, of the Boiling Springs, and a man by the name of Adam Wood lived a near neighbor to them, with whom I formed an acquaintance and entered into an agreement with, that in the event either of our families were attacked, we should render each other every assistance in our power. But a short time elapsed from the period of the said agreement before a band of Tories, passing through that section at night, stopped at Wood's house, killed him, and commenced a general work of destruction, laying waste everything which chanced to be in their way. I distinctly heard the uproar and the firing of arms, and from the direction I knew Wood was attacked. Having retired for the night, I immediately arose, and in company with three others set out for the seat of action. When within a few yards of the house, observing their large and overwhelming numbers, I deemed it prudent to secrete ourselves by the roadside until they had passed. We lay concealed but a few minutes, when, having completed their work of death and desolation, the whole party rode by, two deep. As they passed I counted them, and they numbered one hundred and fifty, headed by those notorious scoundrels, robbers, and murderers, who defeated the gallant Roberts on the Edisto, as before stated, Chaney and Williams. They now made their way for the "Big House," but apparently pressed for time, and finding no one at home (my father's family having taken the precaution, during my absence, to remove therefrom), they proceeded on their course towards Capt. Vince's station, on Savannah River. Believing that they intended an attack upon the fort, I suggested to John Cave, one of my companions, that we had better set out forthwith, and, if possible, head them, and apprise Capt. Vince of his danger. So mounting our fleetest horses, we sallied forth with all possible speed, and after considerable difficulty, threading our way through the swamps, we arrived at the fort just before the break of day. I requested the sentinel to inform the Captain that I had important intelligence to communicate to him, and desired as quick an interview as possible. The Captain returned an answer that he was sick and confined to his bed. I replied that I could take no excuse, sick or well, he must come out directly. This authoritative command brought him forth immediately. I then related to him what had transpired at the Big House, of the enemy's numbers, and of his approach towards that garrison, advising him, at the same time, to evacuate the fort as soon as possible, unless he felt assured of his safety, and of his being able successfully to contend against so formidable a body, tendering, at the same time, our assistance. He stated to us that his force consisted of but twenty-five men, expressed great doubts of his ability to defend himself against such a numerous enemy, and thought it policy to adopt my suggestion to leave the fort, which was agreed on, and in a few minutes the fort was left to the mercy of the enemy, who in the course of one hour afterwards made a charge upon it with his full force, confidently expecting a prize; but instead of a prize they had the sore mortification to find that their deep laid scheme and hellish design on this occasion was completely baffled.

From this point they turned towards their headquarters, on Edisto. In crossing the Lower Three Runs, they stopped at the house of a Mr. Collins, a very quiet and inoffensive man, and far advanced in years, say about eighty-five. Whatever may have been the sentiments of this old gentleman, he maintained a strictly neutral position, shouldering arms on neither side; yet those fiends of darkness dispatched him, with his head as white as snow by the frost of many winters, for an eternal world. How, how could these monsters in human shape dream of prospering, when murdering the aged and inoffensive in this horrid and brutal manner—and why all this bloodshed? Because the honest Whigs of the Revolution, knowing full well the rights of man, and daring to maintain them, refused to be galled by the servile chains of a foreign despot, and to bow submissively to his barbarous impositions. It was this which inspired them with invincible fortitude and zeal, and enabled them to throw off the tyrant yoke, and to declare themselves "free, sovereign, and independent."

I continued scouting both in Georgia and Carolina with very little intermission until the British, under Sir Henry Clinton, took Charleston, with Gen. Lincoln's army of 4,000 men, in 1780—the intelligence of which threw the whole State into consternation and alarm. Our stronghold, with the major part of our army, were now effectually in the hands of the enemy, and those poor deluded wretches, the Tories, by this success of their allies at Charleston, seemed urged on with renewed impetuosity in their cruel and diabolical purposes. And dark indeed were the prospects of the friends of liberty about this juncture; despair was depicted in every countenance; our sun became obscured, and seemed ready to go down to rise no more, and the bird of liberty appeared as if taking its parting gaze of the fertile and flowery region over which it had hovered to plant the tree of liberty—beneath whose bowers the dispersed and oppressed of all nations might find an asylum.

What now to do I knew not. It appeared like madness to remain longer, surrounded by an overwhelming foe, liable at any moment to be butchered without mercy; and to flee the country was almost equally trying—many were pursuing the latter expedient, leaving for other sections where danger was less threatening and where hostilities had scarcely opened. And my brother, Bartlet Brown, and myself thought it advisable for us to pursue the same course, so we returned to Virginia, our native State. In consequence of the scarcity of clothing during the war, we were poorly clad, and in a bad condition to set out on a journey of five hundred miles, and that, too, with but the paltry sum of three dollars in our pockets to defray expenses. On reaching the "Ridge," about seventy miles from home, our little party had augmented to the number of sixty or seventy, all fleeing the country with the same object in view as ourselves. Journeying onward we arrived at Fishing Creek, where we encamped a day or two, not wishing to progress too rapidly for fear of overtaking a detachment of British cavalry under Col. Tarleton, who we learned had been sent by Lord Cornwallis to attack Col. Buford, and had surprised and defeated him at the Waxhaws, and were on their line of march through Charlotte, North Carolina, which lay directly in our route. Whilst encamped at Fishing Creek, a fellow by the name of Mobley, a Tory, came into our camp as a spy. This fellow was so inquisitive, and so particular in examining everybody and everything about the premises, that our suspicions were very much excited in regard to his true character. We, however, suffered him to depart unmolested. And we afterwards learned that he returned to the encampment, at the head of a large gang of Tories, with a view to capture us, but we anticipated his design and escaped from his clutches, being at the distance of fifteen or twenty miles when he made his charge upon the tents. Continuing onward we arrived in sight of Charlotte, when we again encamped, remaining several days. Here many of our party separated from us for different routes, reducing our number to about thirty.

The citizens of Charlotte dispatched a messenger to us, praying that in the event the British, who were marching toward that quarter, attacked the town we would render them assistance. This we promised to do, provided they would furnish us with ammunition, our supply being almost exhausted. On the return of their messenger they sent us a keg of powder and lead in proportion. But at the expiration of three days, waiting for the anticipated attack, the citizens of Charlotte informed us that the enemy had gone back. We then "struck our tents" and resumed our march, taking with us the ammunition sent to us by the citizens of Charlotte, which served us in the place of money, as we could barter it for bacon and corn at the mills as we passed on. Throughout the rest of our journey nothing of importance transpired.

We reached our place of destination in Virginia, our mother country, all safe and sound. Shortly after our arrival there, intelligence was received that depredations and outrages to an alarming extent had been perpetrated in South Carolina, particularly in our own district. The substance of which was that McGeart and his company of Tories crossed the Savannah River from Georgia, at Summerlin's Ferry (now called Stone's Ferry), taking the course of the river, and killing every man he met who had not sworn allegiance to the King. This notorious scoundrel passed in this trip through the neighborhood where my father lived, and brutally murdered seventeen of the inhabitants, among whom were my father, Henry Best, and Moore, leaving John Cave for dead, who afterwards recovered. They burnt my father's house level with the ground, and destroyed everything he possessed—my mother and sisters escaping by fleeing to the woods, in which they concealed themselves until the vile wretches departed. But the work of death did not stop here. This atrocious deed of the sanguinary McGeart and his band was shortly succeeded by another equally, nay, doubly cruel. The British Col. Brown marched down from Augusta with an overwhelming force of Tories and Indians, and taking their stand at "Wiggins' Hill," commenced a slaughter of the inhabitants. The news of which reached the ears of those brave and dauntless officers, Cols. McCoy and Harden, who soon hastened to the defence of the terrified Whigs, and coming upon the enemy, charged upon them and killed and routed them to a man, Col. Brown escaping to the woods. Cols. McCoy and Harden, having accomplished all that was required of them, retired from the field of action, after which Brown returned with the residue of his force and retook the "Hill," at which he remained until he hung five of our brave fellows—Britton Williams, Charles Blunt, and Abraham Smith, the names of the other two not recollected—then he decamped for Augusta. My brother and myself were now in Virginia, among our relations and friends, and would have been as happy as we desired, had it not been for the intelligence from South Carolina, particularly of the section we had left. Hearing that the British, Tories, and Indians had murdered our father and sixteen more of his neighbors, burning to ashes his house and all within it, our mother and sisters escaping to the woods, with little or nothing to support upon, and no male friend to help them, my blood boiled within my veins, and my soul thirsted for vengeance. We now learnt that Gen. Washington had sent an army to the South, under the command of Gen. Gates and Baron DeKalb, and we determined forthwith to set out for the seat of strife we had left. In our journey we passed Anson Court House, N. C., which we found to be a hot bed of Tories. Col. Wade and his company were stationed there, and the Tories were flocking in and rallying under him from all quarters. On the day of our arrival there, a large gang came in, headed by a fellow who doubtless thought he was doing great things for the King and his servile subjects. My mind could but revolve upon their delusion, and the little value they set upon the rich gems of liberty and independence, with which the Whigs were so enamored, and for which they so hard struggled. It has often been a matter of astonishment to me how we escaped the swarm of Tories at Anson C. H. But so it is, we did, and being eager to accomplish our journey and lose no time, we traveled through long and chilling rains, it being in the fall season, exposing ourselves to imminent danger, for the fever raged with great mortality at that time in that region of country. While at Anson C. H. a fellow endeavored to prevail on us to stay all night with him, but from his suspicious appearance we declined his invitation, and declared our intention to pursue our route, notwithstanding the storm that was then raging. On that night, as well as on several preceding ones, we took shelter under large trees in the swamp, our clothes being as wet as water could make them, and our bodies almost chilled through. In the morning it cleared off, and we pursued our journey.

Overtaking General Marion at "Kingstree," Black River, S. C., we immediately united with his troops. Marion's route lay then between the Santee and Little Pedee Rivers; and being desirous to intercept and defeat Col. Watts, who was then marching at the head of four hundred men, between Camden and Georgetown, every arrangement and preparation was made to carry into execution his design. All things being now ready, Watts appeared in sight at the head of his large force, and as

...

they marched down the road with great show and magnificence (hoping, no doubt, to terrify and conquer the country), they spied us; at which time the British horse sallied forth to surround us. Marion, with his characteristic shrewdness and sagacity, discovered their manœuvres, anticipated their object, and retreated to the woods, some four or five hundred yards, and prepared for them. In a few moments they came dashing up, expecting to find us all in confusion and disorder, but to their astonishment, we were ready for the attack, and perceiving this, they called a halt, at which time Marion and Horry ordered a charge. Col. Horry stammered badly, and on this occasion he leaned forward, spurred his horse, waved his sword, and ran fifty or sixty yards, endeavoring to utter the word *charge*, and finding he could not, bawled out, *"Damn it, boys, you, you know what I mean, go on!"*

We were then doing what we could, pressing with all rapidity to the strife, and before the British could get back to the main body, we slew a goodly number of them. Being eager to do all the damage we could, we pursued the fellows very close to the line of the main body, and as soon as they got in, Watts began to thunder his cannon at us, and to tear down the limbs and branches of the trees, which fell about us like hail, but did no other damage than to wound one of our men, Natt. Hutson, and one horse slightly. Marion now finding his force, which consisted only of two hundred men (though sterling to a man, brave, fearless, and patriotic), was too small to give Watts open battle, guarded the bridges and swamps in his route, and annoyed and killed his men as they passed.

For prudence sake, Marion never encamped over two nights in one place, unless at a safe distance from the enemy. He generally commenced the line of march about sunset, continuing through the greater part of the night. By this policy he was enabled effectually to defeat the plans of the British and to strengthen his languishing cause. For while the one army was encamping and resting in calm and listless security, not dreaming of danger, the other, taking advantage of opportunity, and advancing through the sable curtains of the night unobterved, often effectually vanquished and routed their foes. It was from the craftiness and ingenuity of Marion, the celerity with which he moved from post to post, that his enemies gave to him the significant appellation of the "Swamp Fox." Upon him depended almost solely the success of the provincial army of South Carolina, and the sequel has proven how well he performed the trust reposed in him. His genuine love of country and liberty, and his unwearied vigilance and invincible fortitude, coupled with the eminent success which attended him through his brilliant career, has endeared him to the hearts of his countrymen, and the memory of his deeds of valor shall never slumber so long as there is a Carolinian to speak his panegyric.

The heavy rains which prevailed at this time and inundated the country to a considerable extent, proved very favorable to Marion. He now sent a detachment of seventy men, myself one of the number, across the Santee, to attack the enemy stationed at "Scott's Lake" and "Monk's Corner." We crossed the river at night in a small boat, commanded by Captains James and John Postell, dividing our force into two companies, each consisting of thirty-five men. Capt. James Postell took one company and proceeded to "Scott's Lake," but ascertaining the strength of the enemy, and finding the place too well fortified to warrant an attack, he abandoned the project and returned again to the river, and awaited the arrival of Capt. John Postell, who, in the meantime, had marched with the other company to "Monk's Corner." It was my good fortune to accompany the latter. Just about the break of day we charged upon the enemy. Our appearance was so sudden and unexpected that they had not time even to fire a single gun. We took thirty-three prisoners, found twenty odd hogsheads of old spirits, and a large supply of provisions. The former we destroyed, but returned with the latter and our prisoners to the army on Santee. The news of our attack on "Monk's Corner" having reached the enemy at "Scott's Lake," they forthwith marched to their assistance, but arrived too late to extend any—we had captured their comrades, bursted their hogsheads of spirits, gathered their provisions, and decamped before their arrival. Capt. James Postell, being apprised of their march to assist their friends at "Monk's Corner," returned to the fort, set fire to it, and burned it level to the ground.

Shortly after this circumstance one of our most efficient officers, Col. Harden (whom I have before mentioned as having had an important engagement with Brown at "Wiggins' Hill"), joined the army under Marion, as also did Major Snipes, who had recently made a miraculous escape from the Tories through the faithfulness of his negro man, Cudjo. Major Snipes related the whole circumstance to me, and displayed the blisters upon his body, occasioned by the intense heat of the flames from the house set on fire by the Tories as he lay concealed in a brier patch close by, a particular account of which may be seen in Horry's life of General Marion.

On the 1st day of April, 1780, I left Gen. Marion on the Big Pedee River, in company with eighty others, forming a detachment under the command of Cols. Harden and Baker, and Major John Cooper. The two last mentioned officers were from Midway settlement, Georgia. There were also several other brave and energetic men who rendered themselves conspicuous in the war in our detachment, Fountain Stewart, Robert Salley, the Sharps and Goldings, from Georgia. Our route lay by the "Four Holes." Crossing the Edisto at Givham's Ferry, we fell in with a man who assisted Brown in hanging the five brave fellows at "Wiggins' Hill." We gave him his due, and left his body at the disposal of the birds and wild beasts. Pursuing our march, we came to "Red Hill." within about two miles of Patterson's Bridge, Saltkatchie. It was now in the night, but the moon being in full strength, and not a cloud to darken her rays, it was almost as bright as day. Near this place were stationed a body of Tories, commanded by Capt. Barton. They were desperate fellows, killing, plundering, and robbing the inhabitants without mercy or feeling. A company of men, commanded by Major Cooper, were now sent to see what they could do with those murderers. In a few minutes after their departure we heard them fighting, which continued for nearly one hour, when Cooper returned and told us he had killed the greater part of them, with but the loss of one man, John Steward, from Georgia.

We then proceeded on for Pocataligo. Soon after we left Red Hill we entered upon a long, high causeway; a man came meeting us and told us Col. Fenwick, with the British horse, were marching on just behind. We paid no attention to him, not knowing who he was, but went ahead; however, we did not go many rods before the advance parties met and hailed each other—a charge was now ordered on both sides, and we directly came together on the causeway, which was so high that there was no getting off on either side, so a fight was inevitable, and at it we went like bull dogs. The British at length made their way through, though they found it tough work in doing so. We put one of their men to his final sleep on the causeway, and wounded eight more badly, one of whom they had to leave on the road. They wounded one of our men, Capt. James Moore, in thirteen places, though very slightly, and two others who never laid up for their wounds.

We now lay by for two or three days, and then marched for the fort at Pocataligo. When we came in sight of it, I took thirteen of the best mounted men to survey the premises, and to lead them out if possible. When we had got within about two hundred yards of Bambifer's house, where the British had deposited their wounded, I saw a negro run in the house, and immediately I saw several men running for the fort; we struck spurs to our horses, and soon came up with them and took them prisoners. When we had gotten them to our company, we found them to be Cols. Fennick and Leachmore, who had been out to see their wounded. When we arrived at the fort, we had not the smallest hope of taking it, but now finding we had two of their most efficient officers [Major Andrew Devo the only one in the fort], Cols. Harden and Baker sent a flag in for them to give up the fort. When the flag was passing by Col. Fennick, he asked what that meant. On being told it was for them to surrender the fort, he ripped and swore, and hoped "that if they did surrender it, they might all be in hell before the morrow."

After deliberation in the fort for the space of two hours, they all marched out, well armed, tied their horses to what was then called "Abatis," advanced some little distance from the fort, and formed a line. We then marched between them and the fort and took them prisoners—they having one hundred and ten men and we eighty. If all the men in the fort had been brave and true to their cause, I don't think one thousand men could have taken them, for the fort was advantageously located and well fortified, approachable only at three points, all of which were well guarded by a deep creek and cannons. Part of the men in the fort were as good Whigs as we had—Col. Stafford, Col. Davis, Capts. Felts and Green, whose son was with us, also others. We now paroled the prisoners and sent them to Charleston, then burnt the house and leveled the fort with the ground. Next day Col. McCoy, who had been outlaying, came down to us, and my brother Bartlett and myself left Col. Harden and came off with him. On our way we called in at old Mr. Hext's, at Coosawhatchie, the father of the late Lawrence Hext, of the Boiling Springs, Beaufort District. After we left Mr. Hext's, and had progressed some distance, a young man behind us, named Wald, whose horse was jaded and traveled slowly, met Ned Williams with a gang of Tories, who asked him who those were that turned up the lane. He told them that it was Col. McCoy and his company, and that the fort at Pocataligo was taken. They then broke for the Saltkatchie. Wald now came up and told us the circumstance, and we immediately pushed after them, and followed them into the Saltkatchie Swamp, but could not overtake them. We returned, got dinner, and encamped that night near the water pond, on the side next to Capt. John Cater's Boiling Springs, in a pine thicket, a little below the springs. Next morning we went up to the "Big House," now belonging to Col. Hay, and there found those of my father's family that the Tories and Indians had left, whom we had not seen before for twelve months. To describe the joy of that meeting is inexpressible;

we now beheld some of those, who were endeared to us by the strongest ties of nature, whom we never expected to see again this side of eternity's ocean, thinking they had fallen victims to the awful storm of war which had been, and was then, raging. Here we could have remained with them, and gladly toiled and labored for their comfort and happiness, but such was our country's great demand for services, we could only stay a few moments with them.

Bidding them farewell, with no hope of meeting them again, we marched for the siege of Augusta. On our way up, we learned that Col. Brown's (a Tory) boats were going up the Savannah River. We went in pursuit of them, and attacked them about opposite the place of the late Stephen Smith, of Savannah River, but they got on the Georgia side, and we could do nothing with them. From this we marched to Augusta, where we met Gens. Pinckney and Twiggs, and commenced the work of extermination. The first attack we made was on the fort at Silver Bluff, now the property of Gov. Hammond, of South Carolina. Brown's boats had now arrived, and stowed away their goods in the fort. The British not being willing to yield without a struggle, we stove a cannon ball through the brick house in the fort, and they immediately marched out and surrendered, for fear we would serve them the like trick.

The next fort we attacked was that commanded by the wretched Grason, at the upper end of the town. This we soon stormed and took—Capt. Alexander shooting Grason for his villainous conduct in the country. Some made their escape from us by fleeing to Brown's fort, near the river. Before we laid siege to Brown's fort, a fellow by the name of Rutherford (a villain withal) took a company and slipped out in the night down the river, opposite Beech Island, and just at the break of day surprised our horse guard. It being in the bend of the river, the British and Tories got round them, and having a superior force, our men took to the river, but they killed several of our brave fellows while they were swimming, some making their escape—my brother, Bartlett Brown, was one among that number. We heard of their trip after our guard, and pushed to cut them off, but were too late by a few moments only, for as we got within one hundred and fifty yards of the lane, we saw them enter. A few moments sooner, and we would have fixed them snugly.

We now commenced the siege of Brown's fort. In taking this fort, we had great difficulty. We raised a platform fifteen or twenty feet high, and mounted a cannon upon it, and from thence fired at them in the fort. In this way we destroyed a good many of them, but finding we were too hard for them in this way, and to screen themselves from the thunder and lightning of our platform, they dug several caves in the sides of the walls of the fort and crawled into them. We then continued the entrenchment, and as we entrenched, we rolled up cowhides and placed them on the embankment for portholes to shoot through. One morning I was standing next to young Stafford, who was about to shoot through one of our portholes, and there came a ball from the fort and killed him dead. Young Stafford was with me in Gen. Marion's army, and he was, indeed, a brave and patriotic fellow, and dying in freedom's cause, his memory should never fade from our recollection. Before Brown would surrender, we entrenched so near his fort that I could run a hoe-helve from the entrenchment into the fort. On finding we were so near upon him, he marched out and surrendered with all his force and goods. Brown had been such a desperate fellow, there existed great anxiety to kill him; but as he came under the capitulation, we had no chance to do so at this time, but I determined to do so on his way down the river. I took a few brave fellows, and slipped down the river to carry into execution my determination, but he made his escape, through the shades of the night, in a small canoe.

When we commenced the siege of Augusta it was the 1st of April, 1781; when we closed it was the 1st of the ensuing August. Having labored so hard and incessantly to dig Brown out of his fort, I concluded when I had done so to take a peep into it, but it was a sore peep to me, as I took the small-pox from it. I now went home very sick, and as none of our family had ever had it, I had to take the woods—so I retreated back of the Big House to an old field, next to the swamp, under a large oak tree. The weather being very hot, I suffered intensely. While there I employed one Peggy Ogleby to be my nurse. This slut was a Tory, and informed her clan where I was. They said they would come and kill the d—n rebel, but as I had an invisible and Almighty Protector, they had not the power to execute their malicious design. If I am not mistaken, the period I lay under that oak was forty days. When I recovered I joined Major Cooper, at Beech Island, and we continued scouting until the end of the war, in December, 1782. I then returned home, but the British and Tories had nearly destroyed everything we possessed. My mother lived but a short time after the close of the war, and the estate she left each child was thirty-nine pounds ten shillings, sterling.

Although the war had closed, the Tories were still troublesome, plundering and occasionally killing the inhabitants. The foremost scoundrels in this diabolical work were John Black, Zekiel Maulfers, Lark Loudon, and two others, whose names I will not mention as they have relations in the country, who could not help what they did. These fellows murdered a good man at Cherry Hill, Ga., for which John Black and the two whose names are not mentioned, were killed and hung at Savannah; the other two, the worst of the clan, made their escape to Carolina, where they murdered and plundered until the citizens were afraid to travel the roads, day or night. Finding the Whigs were upon the lookout for them, they stole Judge Haywood's match horses and five negroes, and horses from various persons, and started for the Western country.

I heard of their crossing the ridge, and being unwilling they should escape with impunity, I got three other men, Richard Simmons, Gill Thomas, and Benjamin Brown, and put out after them. We pursued them into East Tennessee—over Watorger, we came upon them and took them prisoners. It was now in the month of January, and extremely cold; the snow was on the ground two feet deep, and withal, I had the measles very badly. What to do I hardly knew. I concluded, however, to

risk the consequences, and bidding farewell to these cold and
frozen regions, I began to retrace my steps with my prisoners
and their plunder. We crossed the Watorger on the ice, and
when we had gotten on the Yellow Mountains, it snowed again
and freezed on the top, so that a passage through it was very
difficult. We had to force our way by changing the foremost
horse every hundred yards. Just as we got to the turn in the
mountain night overtook us, so we encamped for the night,
building our fire out of the chestnut limbs on the snow. Next
morning we came down to the foot of the mountains to one
Samuel Bright, and got a little dry pumpkin for our breakfast,
the people having little or nothing else to eat. Having so
many prisoners, horses, and negroes, our funds now run out,
so we had to sell what we could spare to defray expenses. We
now came to Pad. Bryant's, where these runaways had left one
of Judge Haywood's horses, which we got, and tarried all
night. It was indeed a dark and rainy night, and the prisoners
thought to take an advantage of us by it, so they framed an
excuse to go out. Being handcuffed and tied, I apprehended
no danger, but I took one of my company along with me.
They had, unperceived, loosed the rope under the blankets.
It was in an old field, on the slant of a hill, and when we had
gotten out they started to run down the hill. My gun being
loaded with buck-shot, I fired at one of them and stuck one
shot in his ancle, his foot being up at the crack of the gun, the
shot run up into the calf of his leg, but it did not bring him
to the ground. Being young and active, I now threw down my
gun and pushed after him, and just as I was about to take hold
of him I struck a stump, which knocked me over, but I soon
recovered from my fall, and put out after him again; and, as
before, just as I was about to take him the second time, I ran
upon the second stump, which thew me clean over. I now
gave up the chase, as by this time he had gotten too far. Next
morning I had a curiosity to examine the ground I had run
over after these fellows, and I found but the single two stumps
in the way—they had just missed them and I run over both.
We now went in pursuit of these villains, when we soon came

upon one, and in taking him, Simmons put an end to his existence; the other was taken the next day, and put in the 96th District prison. When we had gotten home we sent for him, and he was carried to Beaufort, where there were seven indictments against him. He was tried, condemned and hung.

On the delivery of Judge Haywood's horses to him, he gave me twenty-five guineas, not only for his horses, but also for putting a stop to the outrages of these villains. The other persons whose property we brought back gave us five guineas apiece, and the public gave us twenty-five pounds sterling.

Some time after the close of these things, I married and settled myself between the Sand Hill and Cedar branches, waters of the Lower Three Runs, Barnwell District. On each of these streams I built mills, and from the mills, between which I lived, I gave my place the name of "Fork Mills." The mills are now owned by Major Wm. H. Peyton, my son-in-law. From this place I moved to Boiling Springs, where I have lived and enjoyed fine health for many years, and where I expect to die, if I die at home. I have followed the delightful business of farming ever since the close of the war, and the Lord has been pleased to grant me enough of the good things of this life to keep me free from want down to the present moment.